HOW TO BE
AN AMERICAN

AN OFF-THE-RECORD
GUIDE FOR HOW TO BE
AN IMMIGRANT IN
AMERICA

Satish Mehta

Disclaimer
This is a satirical book for educational and
entertainment purposes only. The views expressed are
those of the author alone. The reader is responsible
for his or her own conclusions and actions. Adherence
to all applicable laws and regulations, including
international, federal, state, and local governing
professional licensing, business practices, advertising,
and all other aspects of doing business in the United
States, Canada, or any other jurisdiction is the sole
responsibility of the purchaser or reader. Neither the
author nor the publisher assumes any responsibility
or liability whatsoever on behalf of the purchaser or
reader of these materials.
ISBN: 9781080938551
Published in Tampa, Florida by Dhaakar, LLC
Library of Congress Cataloging – in – Publication
Data is available

Dedication

To my amazing friends at Edward's Pipe and Tobacco shop, what would I do without you? That is a rhetorical question. I do not want to find out. Thank you for giving me lessons in wry and sometimes sarcastic humor.

Reviews

"Read your new book in one sitting. Irreverently funny, but like all good satire: much truth to be found. ... A terrific book: I enjoyed your work and learned."

Rufus J. Williams 111
Cardinal Point Advisors LLC Principal

"Although My experience has been different in some aspects covered in this book, I thoroughly enjoyed reading a different perspective. The topics covered, I imagine, could be extremely valuable to a new immigrant to our country. I didn't realize how important the conversation about the weather really could be."

Josh Taylor
Fortune 500 company
Senior Compliance Officer.

"How to Be an American," is meant to be a tongue-in-cheek primer for immigrant assimilation; it certainly achieves this goal as well as being a fun-house mirror for US citizens. In reading this, I had more than a few chuckles at myself and fellows. I am sure that many of us have not thought about how we look in the eyes of other cultures; the comparisons herein may be an eye-opener for those less aware of the differences between different cultures, and in some cases the, similarities. The rule here is: Never take yourself too seriously. Altogether a delightful read.

~Joseph L. Lennox-Smith, M.Ed., Ph.D.(abd)

Contents

Preface

The reception to the theme of this book when I first mentioned it to the people at Edward's Pipe and Tobacco was at once a pleasant surprise and a disappointment for me. A surprise, because the reception was so encouraging; a bummer for the same reason. Here is what I mean.

Those familiar with the writing and the publishing trade will realize that it is impressive, excuse me, I need to be a bit more Southern: a not entirely ordinary thing for a completely unknown author and an immigrant with a native language different than English, to write three books in about two years. What is my problem then?

Well, writing books has completely changed the image I had of myself. My book, "A Pig in the Python," was to be a book about boldness. Before its release, I was a man on a mission to tell the Americans what to do. I had spoken my mind without fear of repercussions. I thought I was courageous, outspoken, and expected to either go unnoticed or confront some significant consequences. No storm came. I expected my friends at the store to be outraged against me, but they patted me on the back. I thought that they would rise in rage, but all they said was, "you are a liberal." It was, indeed a big disappointment.

While many will be quick to typecast "How to be an American" as an anti-American discourse, my enlightened readers will enjoy the light-hearted, slightly satirical guide and could benefit immensely from reading this book while settling in this country. I want the immigrants to see America in its right light. This could be hard to bear for some people because it may not always be the most favorable light. However, it is a very human light, and that itself is the most desirable aspect.

A few days after the publication of "A Pig in the Python," I felt better when I heard from a retired senior executive of a Fortune 50 company. He sat in a comfortable lounge chair by the pool and went through the book without a break. While reading, he continually puffed and smoked two Rocky Patel cigars all the way to the end. When he finished reading, the old man stood up with a burst of energy and shouted:

"Blatant disrespect!"

Then he threw the book into the pool where it hit his wrinkled-skinned, skinny-dipping girlfriend on the butt.

He is an old-style, conservative, and a patriotic soul, and he did me a big favor. I wish there were more like him in Florida. I have not come across another so far. Since his feedback, I have decided to stay away from socio-political and economic topics and focus more on the lighter things that make America the country it is.

I am enjoying writing, "How to be an American." It will do well for me. I can be myself, a slightly satirical commentator.

I published my first two books on Amazon's KDP platform. Not too many know about them. The key is marketing, something I do not have the money to afford. This time, I am planning to take this manuscript to a childhood friend of mine. He owns a publishing company. If he does not get too many scripts from better-known authors, he may accept it. It is also possible that my friend will want to buy all the rights to my past and future books at my price! Hey, in America, I do have a right to dream!

Satish Mehta   June 14, 2019

Introduction

My friends at Edward's Pipe and Tobacco believe that I am uniquely qualified to write a book on how to be an immigrant in America. I am an immigrant myself. What is more, I am also the son of parents who, during the partition of India and barbaric violence in Pakistan, took refuge in New Delhi, India. I was born in India, and I grew up in a city full of immigrants. I did not notice anything particular or irregular about myself. Then I came to the U.S., and you can imagine my awkward surprise.

Like all life-changing discoveries, it was a matter of a few seconds. Here is how it happened.

As an MBA student, I spent a lot of time with a young woman who was a proud American. Her ancestors had migrated to the U.S. in the early 1950s from Hungary. Once she asked me—to my great surprise—if I would marry her. "No," I answered. "I shall not. My parents would never support my marrying an alien." She looked at me a little confused and irritated, and retorted, "I, an alien? Are you out of your f-----g mind? I am an American. You are the foreigner. And your parents, too." Hey, I am not the type to give in. "They are in New Delhi, India. There too?" I exclaimed. "Everywhere," she stated authoritatively. "Truth does not depend on geography. What is true in the U.S. is also true in India and China and Russia and everywhere."

I immediately recognized that her philosophy was as indisputable as it was simple.

It is disgraceful and in poor taste to be an immigrant. It is hopeless to pretend any different. There is no way out. A convict may improve and become a decent member of American society. An immigrant cannot recover. Once an immigrant, always an immigrant. There is no way out for her. She may become an American citizen; she can never become American.

Therefore, it is better to accept the sad reality. Some gracious Americans might forgive you. Others may see this as not your fault, only your misfortune. They will treat you with disdain, understanding, and sympathy. They will invite you to their homes. Just as lap dogs and other pets, they are quite prepared to keep a few immigrants.

This book, *"How to be an American"* therefore expresses more than it should. How to be an immigrant in America? One should not be an immigrant at all. There are mostly unwritten but specific guidelines and manners, however, which you must know if you want to make yourself as tolerable and cultured as you possibly can.

Learn these rules and imitate the Americans. If you do not succeed in emulating them, you will look absurd, although if you do, you run the risk of even looking more absurd.

America Then And Today

I hear many say that the U.S. of today is vastly different from the U.S. of the early 1970s when I came to this country.

In the early 1970s, Americans were tall, big, and friendly. Today, they are tall, big, and warm. Then, they were jovial, a little loud and fun to be with. Today they are jovial, lively, and fun to be with. Then, they were honest, likable, and compassionate. Today they are sincere (politicians and media excluded), amiable, and kind. Then, they kept discussing "how to attract the opposite sex" excitedly. Today they keep debating "how to attract the opposite sex" more excitedly. Then, their main interests were baseball, football, and cars, while today, their core interests are pets, cars, and football. Then, TV topics were a comedy, sex, and money. Today it is money, sex, and more sex.

In the early 1970s, there were not too many immigrants from South Asia. Americans were inquisitive about this new breed from mysterious lands. Today Americans can recognize Asian Indians from afar and are quite knowledgeable about Indian culture, cuisine, and values.

Until recent years, a vast number of Americans toured Europe. They loved investigating their roots and enjoyed the hospitality. They still travel to Europe, but now they also travel to Asia and frequently go on Caribbean cruises.

Then, there were some Americans traveling to the Far East (China and Japan). Most Americans now know that there are other countries in Asia besides China and Japan. Then, Americans went out to eat at European restaurants, diners serving continental food, and occasionally to a Chinese eatery. Today they enjoy a large variety of Asian cuisine including Indian, Thai, Malaysian, Chinese and Japanese. If an American goes out with an Indian friend, she frequently insists on going to an Indian restaurant. They claim to love Indian food. Sometimes, it is the truth.

Then, cars were huge and made of steel. Gas was cheap. Americans bought only American cars. When they discovered that other countries also made cars, Americans just assumed them to be of lower quality and toy-sized. Today, imported cars are the majority in the U.S.

In those days, the color TV was still the "in" thing. Telephones were immobile but had long cords. We inserted coins in the jukebox at a diner to listen to the music. We read books, newspapers, and tabloids. We made necessary phone calls from public phone booths. Now we have the Internet, electronic readers, laptop computers, robots, and smartphones with apps for knowing or doing everything. Then, Americans prayed to God for answers. Now, they Google it.

Many earlier generations remember the proverbial "good old days." The technological advances in the last five decades have changed the lifestyle. We have more leisure time, productivity has zoomed, healthcare although expensive, is at its best. What has not changed is the friendly and welcoming American culture. These are the best of times.

Which America?

When Americans say America, they sometimes mean the North, sometimes the Midlands, sometimes the West, and sometimes the Deep South— but hardly ever the United States of America. Unless you are watching people eating mere hot dogs, the culture is different in each area.

On Sundays in the state of Mississippi, even the most unfortunate person puts on his best suit or dress, tries to look respectable, and celebrates his blessed life. In Vermont on Sundays, even the wealthiest person puts on jeans or sweats, lets his hair loose or uncombed, does not shave, and celebrates his blessed life by trying to look ordinary.

"Keeping up with the Kardashians" dominates TV viewing in California and Arizona. Tennessee, Arkansas, and Mississippi cherish "Duck Dynasty." The state with the largest Mormon population, Utah, loves "Sister Wives." Oklahoma and South Carolina obsess over "Naked and Afraid!"

In the Northeastern and industrial Midwestern states, people frequently talk about the need for government regulation, the value of education, and social services for universal good. In West Virginia and Texas, people value individual liberty more and are highly skeptical of the educated elite. The Deep South fights federal intrusion while accepting the most welfare support and economic assistance.

In Florida, there is little, if any, talk of the weather unless a hurricane is in the forecast. In New Jersey, you are boring if you do not compliment or complain about the weather at least fifty times a day.

In Florida, the local "who's who" frequently visit cigar shops with lounges found in all decent size towns. In New Jersey, you have to conduct an extensive search to find a cigar shop and then pay a membership fee to smoke in its claustrophobic sitting area.

In New Jersey, people walk their dogs in the late afternoon or evening. In Florida, dogs walk their owners all day long.

In New Jersey, people go to the zoo to see alligators or crocodiles. In Florida, people go for a casual drive to meet the reptiles.

In the New York metro area, there are fancy restaurants with excellent food. In the

Tampa metro area, people have table manners.

In the New York metro area, all newcomers (immigrants) at least try to learn to speak English. In Tampa, the local population tries to speak Spanish.

In the Northeast, the education of a person shows. In the Southeast, even well-educated people go the extra mile to hide it.

In the Northeast, a mid-level manager wears brand name attire, drives a fancy car, and talks about billion-dollar deals. In the Southeast, billionaires wear jeans and polo shirts and play dominos at cigar shops.

In the Northeast, humor is subtle and sarcastic. Jeff Foxworthy's "You might be a redneck" jokes and Larry the Cable Guy's southern trucker persona relate to audiences in the south.

In the Midlantic states, rarely do you see homes with the U.S. flag. In the southeast, a front yard with the U.S. and Confederate flags is a common sight.

In the Midlantic states, people support their stance with research and rationale. In the South, people defend their position by repeating it louder.

In the U.S., almost every southern state, whether small or big, has openly exhibited its disgust and opposition to the welfare and social programs. The north and west regions generate the revenue to support several southern states financially without even calling it a welfare program.

In the Northeast, a small number of people are right-wingers, a small percentage of people are left-wingers, and the rest are the independents. In the south, you find a few independents, and the rest follow the labels faithfully.

People in the northeast tell you the truth or stay mum; in the south, they hardly ever tell the truth, but they would not dream of telling a lie.

Many northerners think life is a game; the southerners believe baseball is a game.

Meeting and Greeting

Learn English

In 1973, as a young adult, I landed at the John F. Kennedy Airport on my way to Boston. I heard a loud announcement that I could not understand at all. I asked the woman behind the TWA counter what was the broadcast. She looked at me with a smile and said, "Oh, some bullshit." Even then, I knew what "bullshit" meant. That was a confidence booster. I suddenly felt that I had a good command of American English.

Test of English as a Foreign Language® (TOEFL) is a standardized exam to measure the English language ability of non-native speakers wishing to enroll in English-speaking universities. Scoring 95 percentile or above on TOEFL is good, but not enough. Why? Like most languages, everyday spoken American English has its own peculiarities.

First, let us look at the homographs, words of similar spelling but with more than one meaning.

Driving on State Highway 24 in Quincy, Illinois, I noticed a giant billboard that read:

"We use this farm to produce, produce." Not familiar with the local commerce, I could not think of what else they could do with that farm. Even New Jersey has some homographs in its public notices. One landfill in southern NJ put up a large sign on State Highway 70. It read, "This dump is full. We refuse more refuse."

Annual canoeing and rowing competition among the Ivy League schools is a well-attended event in Princeton, NJ. A few years ago, the police had cordoned off an area, which is usually open to the public. When asked why, the officer in charge said, "Oh, it is for public safety. There is a row among the oarsmen about how to row."

English is a crazy language, but most languages are. Get a head start. Know that there is no ham in hamburger. The English did not invent English muffins just as the French did not invent French fries.

Not taking English for granted is helpful. Explore its paradoxes. You can make amends, but not one amend, recite at a play and play at a recital! Have noses that run and feet that smell! A slim chance and a fat chance are the same, while a wise man and a wise guy are opposite!

Marvel at the unique delight of the English language in which your house can burn up as it burns down, you can fill in a form by filling it out and, an alarm goes off by going on. When the stars are out, they are visible, but when the lights are out, they are invisible.

English is originally a language of the Brits. It displays the ingenuity of the human race, which, of course, is not a race at all. I can go on forever, but perhaps this will give you an idea of why you must watch American TV to strengthen your spoken American English language.

Rex Harrison, in one of the greatest musicals of all time, "My Fair Lady," says that an Englishman's way of speaking classifies him. Well, an American's style of speaking regionalizes him. The Cajun style English in certain parts of Louisiana brings others to tears. No wonder Rex Harrison felt that the Americans have not spoken English in years!

Accent, Phrases, and Slang

In 1992, my colleague Carol and I had landed at the Shreveport, Louisiana airport. We stopped at the rental car exit to get directions (No GPS or cell phones at that time). We both listened attentively to the African American attendant, nodding periodically. Once out of the lot, I asked Carol to navigate because I really could not comprehend anything the man had said. He was speaking American Cajun English with a different accent. Surprise, Surprise! Carol could not understand a single word, either! For the same reason.

Before my friends at Edward's notice my Indian accent, I have devised a solution. I keep that unlit pipe in my mouth to mumble between my teeth, smile, nod periodically and finish all sentences with sounds like, "ah ha" or question, "isn't it?" Most may not understand much, but they are used to that, and they think I am smart and affable.

Some immigrants try hard to acquire the accent of the region. I have known some who attempted to imitate the Boston accent. The good is that you give the impression of being in the company of the society; the awkward is that continually trying to speak like the locals is arduous. Talk ordinarily, and you may fall out of it. Where are you then?

I love American phrases, expressions, and idioms. They are funny and make the point very succinctly.

Enjoying Thanksgiving dinner with my friend Jerry Romello and his Sicilian American family in San Diego, I learned a few new phrases. This was in 1985. Jerry was a second generation American. He chose the occasion to announce his engagement and intent to marry a slinky young woman. Later Jerry's fiancé left, and we were watching football, when Jerry's dad asked, "Hey, J, every time you meet a girl, you get married. Why? This will be your third marriage. I don't understand why you want to buy a cow when you can get the milk for free!" I understood.

In my first year at college, I picked up a working understanding of frequently used phrases. The next 45 years convinced me decisively that I would never know all of them. Depressing, right? Not necessarily. I console myself with a reminder that nobody knows all of them, and new ones are created daily.

The average American uses about five hundred words. Those with higher education, especially academicians, may approach a vocabulary of about 1000 words. You may learn another 1000 and another 10,000 and yet another 20,000, and still, you may come across a further 20,000 you have never heard of before, and nobody else has either.

American English is somewhat like the universe. Astrophysicists claim that the cosmos is infinite and expanding rapidly. American English has a vast vocabulary, and it is growing continually. What are the impetuses? I am not a linguist. Although I do have a theory.

First, the U.S. absorbs more immigrants than any other country in the world. People have migrated here from Britain, Africa, Ireland, Italy, France, Spain, Portugal, Poland, Germany, Greece, and more recently from India, China, and the Middle East. American English continually assimilates words and expressions from other languages and cultures. Ever heard of "karma?" That is a word from Hindi, the predominant language in India.

Another factor is the natural evolution with each new generation. All generations coin words and slang primarily because they want to create their own identity, express independence, and fit into their social groups. Slang, especially, is always evolving, and in a few years, new weird words will completely replace the current ones.

I tried to slide a few trendy words into my conversation with my sixteen years old niece. She politely advised me not to be so "cringey (awkward),"...and called my attempt to be hip, "extra (over the top)." TBH, my squad is at Edwards Pipe and Tobacco store. It is a fleeky kickback. No one is drippin. Some are ratchet, savage, and of course, there is a lot of throwing shade. No one is a clout chaser or clout demon. It's lit. They are fam. They are woke. If you are shook about the new slang, sip tea.

I guess you get the idea. If not, spend a little more time with teens and young adults.

Introductions

Americans are friendly people. In most towns, strangers will smile and acknowledge you with a "Hi." Of course, you cannot expect to smile at everyone riding with you on a subway in a large city like New York City or Chicago. Some newbies try that but end up with facial cramps.

Americans love their privacy. When introducing people, the idea is not to reveal a person's identity. It is almost essential that you should not pronounce anybody's name in a way that the other party may be able to grasp it.

Never reveal someone's full name. The first name is okay, but disclosing just the nickname is better and a lot more prevalent. Therefore, Rick meets Dick, Joe, Jim, Chuck, Ted, and Phil. Once you are better acquainted, they may tell you their last name.

Americans are ingenious and practical. While the English language is expanding rapidly, there is a shortage of names. Therefore, Americans maximize the use of any title and name variation to its full potential. For example, John Sr., John, Johnny, and John Jr.; twenty similar names and your skills to remember and be able to differentiate new friends will improve tremendously.

And, sometimes John is addressed as Jack. It could be his middle name or his family and friends just want an alternate. If you are confused, do not be. It is perfectly reasonable to ask the person to clarify or repeat. Just do not do it too loudly – only whisper. On the other hand, if your name is non-European, you must be prepared to repeat it a few times, each time do it a little louder but slower.

If somebody introduces you to someone, there are some rules to follow.

If he extends his hand to shake yours, do not immediately grasp it. Smile, look into his eyes and simultaneously estimate the size and strength of his hand. Most likely, his goal is to envelop your hand and squeeze it. Once you have ascertained the safety of your hand, and just before, he withdraws his hand, offer your hand only in time to touch his hand lightly. This way, you have completed the handshake without crushing your hand.

After the initial introduction, if you meet the newly gained friend again, wait for the cue before extending your hand. He may just want to fist bump, which is a lot more hygienic.

After the hand dance, it is a common practice to inquire about each other's current state of material, mental and physical health. A frequent way of doing that is asking,

"How are you?" or, "How is it going?" or "What's up?"

Caution. Your new acquaintance who has made such a concerned inquiry is least interested in listening to your struggles or successes. A dialog like this:

"Hey! How is it going?"

You: "Slow to get up. I missed my yoga class. The back is aching, did not sleep well, that new mattress is not suiting me. The vegetable smoothie has begun to stimulate digestion. Under the circumstances, doing reasonably well."

Well, such an explanation will prompt a formal act of considerately looking at you, nodding when you are talking, maybe even throwing in a "yeah," and still not hearing a single word you say.

The next significant expression to be wary of is, "Glad to meet you." "Good meeting you." This comment is usually a lie. The tone of the delivery and context are critical to observe. You will hear "good meeting you" even if the other person is positively disgusted with you.

You must prepare for one more question. "Where are you from?" Immediately, glance at your skin to confirm the color. If it is other than white, the question refers to your place of origin. It does not matter what age and when you migrated to the U.S. It does not matter if you are a U.S. citizen and have been for the past fifty years. Once an immigrant, always an immigrant. To feel better and save energy, just give a complete answer, "I was born in India and migrated to the U.S. 46 years ago. I just moved from NJ to FL."

During the introduction, do not bow or do any other acrobatic feats that may be a common practice in your culture of origin. Adding suffix "Sun (like in Kubota Sun in Japan)" or "Ji (like in Satish Ji in India)" to somebody's name will cause confusion and maybe ire. Americans do not call each other Mr. or Ms. something in everyday conversation unless there is a generational age difference. There also, calling by the first name is the norm. In a selected context, addressing someone as Mr. or Ms. is construed as you being annoyed with him or her.

Similarly, do not attach a tail of degrees following your name. Unlike what the media portrays, Americans are the opposite of narcissists; they are humble in their daily life.

Speak up when someone calls you a doctor or assumes that you are an engineer, IT professional, owner of a hotel, or some retail operation. Just clarify for them what you do for a living. After that, talk about baseball or football. You will make great friends faster.

So, where do Americans mostly meet for introductions?

Coffee or Tea

You will most likely end up meeting your new acquaintances at a Starbucks, or some other coffee or teashop. These places are always full of patrons. There is frequently a queue. While waiting for your turn, it is a good idea to study carefully, the items listed on the menu board.

Until a few years ago, ordering coffee was quite simple. You had a choice of black coffee or coffee with cream and sugar. Now, ordering coffee is not a straightforward decision. There are dozens of variations. From a plain regular coffee to Caffè Americano, Café Latte, Cappuccino, Espresso, Flat White, Long Black, Macchiato, Mochaccino, Irish Coffee, Vienna, Affogato, and many more.

Americans drink coffee because it reinforces their image of strength. Tea is not consistent with their perception of themselves. Until recently if you ordered tea, you would have caught the shop or restaurant unprepared.

However, unknown to the consumers of coffee, the micro niche marketers were working with food and beverage scientists to inject some complexity to the selection of a hot beverage. They discovered that the majority of the world drinks tea. Straight persuasion to have consumers drink tea was an expensive and risky proposition.

Enter American ingenuity. The prominent experts and concerned industry representatives put their heads together and claim to have experimented and recorded the incredible health benefits of combining certain spices and herbs with what used to be just tea. This naturally aromatic, mostly Darjeeling tea, is now available in tens of medicinal flavors and has quickly become the "in" beverage of the health-conscious American. Aspiring to live an average life of a hundred years, this is especially true for Millennials and younger generations.

There is a tea for almost every common ailment. If you are overstressed, chamomile is there to rescue you. It will also help you sleep better. Digestion issues? No problem. Try some ginger tea. If you are not consuming some type of health-focused tea, you may not be keeping up with healthy habits.

Some self-proclaimed nutrition experts claim that black tea makes memory stronger. The other day—I just mention this as my experience—I got up in the morning and made tea. I knew I was missing something. I replayed the sequence of steps from the day before. Ah! I now remember that I usually have a plain slice of bread with my tea. I decided to get a slice from the pantry. But, then I forgot where I had put the cup of hot tea I had just made.

Once you get your coffee or tea at the shop, the conversation begins.

The Art of Conversation

While at a coffee shop in Tampa, I could not help but eavesdrop on this young, attractive couple. They were deeply in love—judging from the way they picked up their own coffees without letting each other's hand go. The young woman lived in Tallahassee, Florida, and her boyfriend in Tampa. These two—because of the distance involved, close to 278 miles—had not personally met since they began dating online over a year ago. Their first in-person meeting appeared to be a happy and loving occasion. Online, they had so much to tell each other that they often stayed up chatting until after midnight. This conversation:

Man, "When I was out on an errand before, I realized how hot it is today."

Woman, "Yes, definitely. I really think so."

Man, "I don't like such hot weather. Not when it is so humid."

Woman, "No. Not at all. Not when it is so humid. I couldn't agree with you more. Not such high temperatures."

Man, "You also get such high temperature in Tallahassee, right?"

Woman, "A fair amount. We get our share of hot weather. You know how it is. One has to take extremely hot with good weather."

Man, "I like hot weather without humidity. Dry heat is fun."

Woman, "Oh, yes. I do enjoy dry heat; you know hot weather but low humidity. Tallahassee often gets hot weather without high humidity."

Man, "I couldn't agree with you more. Not too humid. But we can't complain. It is much better than the snowstorms in the North.

Woman, "No. No need to complain. It is much better than Northern states."

Man, "Yes, it is much better. Right?"

Woman, "Oh, yes. Definitely. I couldn't agree with you more."

Man, "Yes."

Woman, "Yup."

In my opinion, the Internet and smartphones are not killing the art of conversation fast enough. A whole lot of it is still dulling the minds of Americans. I listened for another 30 minutes, and then I pulled out the smartphone from my pocket and yelled, "I am hungry for entertaining and intellectually stimulating news! SNL for me!"

Okay. I grant you that most conversations are more exciting and people are livelier. But, watch your style of talking!

__Talking Style__

Being Smart

"You Asians are so smart," said one of my acquaintances at the Edwards Pipe and Cigar Shop. First, thinking about the vast number of Asian (Chinese, Indian, Koreans, Japanese, Thai, Malaysians, Indonesians, Vietnamese, and the list goes on) idiots and nitwits I have had the pleasure of meeting, I considered this remark overstated but complimentary.

Having thought about it a little more, the comment is far from flattering. The person at the shop could have been condescending, and camouflaging his disdain for the Asian immigrants. After all, there are close to 4.5 billion Asians on this planet. The likelihood of them all being smart is not high.

Americans are polite and generous in handing out compliments, especially when you are a recent acquaintance or a friend. Listen carefully and try to understand a tribute. If you have the slightest doubt, ask them to help you appreciate it.

I googled the word "smart." Most sources define it the same way. For example, the Merriam-Webster dictionary gives seven definitions of "smart"—causing a sharp stinging, marked by vigorous strength, brisk, bright, knowledgeable, shrewd, cunning (bold), neat (trim, stylish, elegant, sophisticated taste, characteristic of contemporary society), guided (automation).

When a person is irritating because they behave as if they know everything, he is called "smart-aleck." That young Indian IT immigrant, Alok, on a temporary visa to the U.S., was thrilled when his boss called him "smart-aleck," confusing "aleck" with "Alok."

At a grocery store in Tampa, I overheard an Indian immigrant saying to the checkout counter cashier, "I am not that able at math, please correct me if I am wrong, but I think that $37.62 multiplied by 73.47 is 2,763.94. I am trying to figure out how much I spent on grocery in Indian rupees." Now, that is not "smart."

An average American knows little about how people live in various parts of the world and what they eat. But, it is not smart to voluntarily state that Indians do not live on trees, and most of them are not surviving on hay and herbs. However, if you mention it anyway and your American friend happens to know that most Indians are carnivorous, she would most likely pretend to be baffled to find out unexpectedly that the Indians live in brick houses too.

It is so much smarter to talk about the Philippines, Guam, Puerto Rico, Samoa or U.S. Virgin Islands—those little countries ...Are they American colonies? (They used to be. Some still are.)

No matter how smart you are and what you want to say, just state it politely. Always be polite. That is very American.

Being Impolite

Joey, a young Italian American (in his late twenties) and I ended up at one of the de facto nude beaches near New York City. Most sunbathers were well toned, enjoying the bright sun. But, then a few wrinkled-skinned older people joined the otherwise good-looking beach lovers. Joey did not miss a beat. He proudly announced to the new group that he was from Silicon Valley and that he had invented a lukewarm, "steamless iron" that could easily make their skin wrinkle-free.

It is easy to be offensive in certain cultures. You just have to say something that is not locally acceptable. In other cultures, it may generate laughter. In the U.S., coarseness has quite a different modus operandi.

In India, if someone tells you a blatant lie, you will respond, "You are a liar. Get out of here." In America, people just say, "Oh, is that so?" Or "That is rather an unusual account, isn't it?"

My daughter and I were at the horse races at the Meadowlands Racetrack in New Jersey. There, I ran into one of my book club buddies, Greg, who is an author with limited writing abilities. But, Greg is most successful at picking the winning horse. After the races, driving back home, my daughter remarked, "What a spendthrift! All the money your author friend makes on diligent racetrack gambling during the weekend, he spends on his writing during the weekdays."

The immigrants face two gaps with their children born in the U.S. There is the generation gap. Add to that the cultural divide. It is complicated yet amusing as well.

An Indian American woman had gained a significant amount of weight. Her husband told her that she was fat. Their seven years old daughter quickly corrected her father, "Mom is not fat! She is just horizontally challenged."

Sometimes by staying silent and letting the other person win, it is not only polite but also to your benefit in the longer term.

As an MBA student with a technical undergraduate degree, I had a decent vocabulary of technical and semi-technical words. Once in an Operations Research class, the lecturer challengingly asked, "So, what does orthogonal mean?" Of course, I knew it meant perpendicular. But, my intuition told me to be silent. Let the lecturer win. This is the question of his pride, he wants to be seen right. In the longer term, it did help me maintain an excellent relationship with the lecturer.

Some years ago, a temporary placement company had a person apply for a "word processing" job at my company. The candidate had seen a computer before and could type ten words a minute, with a whole lot of errors. I had learned the American ways. I gently stated, "I believe you would be a good candidate after you have strengthened your typing skills at higher speeds." This expressed in my native language would be, "Throw this incompetent person out on the street!"

Historically, when a loudmouth and impish citizen annoyed the King of Saudi Arabia or the Ayatollah of Iran, he had his body dismembered without much publicity. But, when the same happens in the U.S., the White House Correspondents' Association invites her to its annual shindig to perform a political comedy routine satirizing the White House administration. Sometimes, when the President is not amused, the whole media and the nation express their immense pride in the First Amendment in the Constitution of the United States of America.

The impolite expressions, when pronounced sternly include, "I am sorry, but...," "Nothing personal ...," "I am afraid...," "How strange that ..." Sometimes you do hear rather crude remarks such as, "Keep your trap shut!" Or "Idiot!" Or "You better complete this!" Such outbursts are wholly un-American, and most likely, the results of immigrants' influence dating back to an unknown era.

Americans prefer negotiation to confrontation. And, they are always negotiating.

Always Negotiating

In every interaction, either you are talking others into doing what you want, or they are convincing you into doing what they want. This type of exchange is continual and often goes unnoticed. But, this is negotiating in its most basic form. Americans recognize this better than most in the world.

However, Americans do not necessarily practice the proverbial "win-win" concept. In my experience, "Win-Win" is the most overused and misused concept spread by theoretic geniuses.

America's number two passion is competitive sports—football, baseball, basketball, golf, tennis, and swimming. There is always a winning side and a losing side. No "win-win" here. It has to be "win-lose," or they will not have sold out stadiums of fans and sports will not be one of the highest revenue producing industries in the United States.

"Everything is Negotiable," is another myth propagated by delusional, self-proclaimed experts. The police do not negotiate with terrorists or kidnappers. There is only one acceptable outcome—never in favor of the criminals. Do not even try to negotiate somebody's faith (religion). Doing so, you run an extraordinary risk of severe mental and physical injuries.

Persuading Americans is complicated because they are well informed but also uninformed. I have seen immigrants repeating what they said earlier, just louder. You may repeat it once hoping that the other person may become enlightened and see it your way. If you do it more than once, the other person will usually ignore you.

Americans do not like to reveal their problems, at least not crisply. Under such circumstances, an immigrant of unexceptional intellect can either be a Tibetan monk and practice silence or be a prudent American and ask the right questions succinctly.

After a decade of hard work, Ali, my Malaysian immigrant friend, could afford a lawn care service. He parked his tractor lawn mower with a big "for sale" sign in the front yard. A middle-aged man in a pick-up truck stopped by and began visually inspecting the tractor.

The prospective buyer asked, "How much?"

"Eight hundred, if I have to deliver it to your place," replied Ali.

"Yeah, I have a little problem," muttered the buyer.

Ali, "I will take six hundred if you pick it up."

"Yeah, but there is a problem," the buyer mumbled.

"Hey, it is a good deal. I have maintained the machine well. But, I will take five hundred if you buy it now," said Ali.

The buyer shook his head, indicating he still had a problem. Finally, Ali asked a good question. "What is the problem? If you tell me what your problem is, maybe I can help you find a solution."

"Well, I don't have cash with me. I can write you a check. I don't mind picking up the tractor after you have cashed the check."

Ali should have asked the right question at the beginning of the conversation.

Several immigrants from the eastern hemisphere claim to be great negotiators. Some of them teach a program on negotiation in prominent business schools. Observe them lecture students in a negotiation class, or watch their "YouTube" tutorials, and you will see the academic brilliance. They assert that all negotiating is trading. You give away items of less importance to you to get what is more relevant to you. In everyday life, they do not walk the talk. Why? What is the problem? Haggling. Haggling is the favorite pastime and staple brain food of most immigrants from the East.

A little rain never stopped Indian immigrants from crowding Oak Tree Road in Iselin, New Jersey. I heard an Indian doctor haggling with an African American vendor selling umbrellas on the sidewalk.

"It is raining. I need one. How much?"
"Three dollars," replied the vendor.
"Naw. Too high. I can't afford it."
"You are wet, man. I have not sold any today. I will give it to you for half off—one dollar and fifty cents."
"It is just water. I can catch a cold, but I will not die. Too expensive."
"You are all wet. I do not want you to fall sick. I will give it to you for free."
"You are a good man! I will take two."

Americans recognize that a certain amount of flexibility is necessary for negotiating and therefore, are proficient compromisers. For instance, all American politics is an eternal, non-compromising battle between compromising Democrats and compromising Republicans.

So, what do Americans mostly talk about?

Talking Topics

Weather

I was walking along the chain of restaurants and quaint shops on North Beach Drive in St. Petersburg, Florida when I ran into Regis, my new cigar buddy at the Edwards Pipe and Tobacco shop.

"Lovely day, isn't it?"
"Isn't it beautiful?"
"Not humid and the sun, just right."
"Isn't it gorgeous?"
"Delightful, isn't it?"
"It's so nice and hot, yet not so hot."
"To me, this is the nicest weather, isn't it?"
"I love it. Don't you?"
"Paradise."

Whether you are meeting the first time or are a long time acquaintance, the weather is one of the most discussed subjects in this vast country. Before I get into describing a different conversation about the weather with a friend in Princeton during Christmas, let me tell you that the stereotyping of climate as a boring or dull subject is unfair. Frequently you hear someone saying, "We discussed weather at the meeting," implying that the meeting was boring and non-productive. Yet, the weather consistently makes the headline news. As I write this book, New Jersey is digging out of five inches of snow; California is still trying to contain the biggest fire in the state's history leaving a large number of human and material casualties; Florida just faced a significant temperature swing from burning hot to cold (but, of course, no snow). I am sure hurricanes or tornados are forming somewhere in or around the country.

America is a people-oriented society, segmented by profession, and strictly focused on their specific needs. You don't have to take my word for it, just listen to the weather forecasts, especially on TV or radio. The weather forecast for specific audiences is different. I have heard predictions like this in eastern Pennsylvania:

"Tomorrow it will be a warm day with low humidity; a lot of sunshine intercepted by scattered clouds for long periods."

Then:

"Weather forecast for the ski enthusiasts. Tomorrow it will be around twenty to thirty degrees Fahrenheit. The light snow overnight will lay a continual layer of soft powder that will keep the skiers floating downhill."

Climate migration is the real culprit of apparently conflicting weather forecasts. Caravans of cold fronts wake up and decide to migrate from North (Canada and up) to the South. Columns of warm fronts from South America display a similar behavior and choose to move North and relocate to the U.S. I do not really understand these caravans of climate fronts and their motives, but even so, I just do not like caravans.

Kevin and I decided to meet at Panera's in Princeton for an evening espresso. The place was packed, people were cheerful, and Christmas carols were playing in the background.

"Nasty day, isn't it?"
"Isn't it crummy?"
"The sleet ...I hate sleet and cold rain."
"I don't like it at all. Do you?"
"Pleasant in the morning, then a bit of rain, and then cold, sleet, sleet, sleet, all day long for the whole week."
"I recall similar weather in 1992."
"Yes. I remember it too."
"Or was it in 1993?"

"Yes, it was."

"Or in 1991?"

"Yes, that's right."

"I like changing seasons. It is better than Florida."

"Absolutely!"

An important principle emerges. You are better off not contradicting anybody when discussing the weather. Should it sleet and snow, should hurricanes, tornadoes, or typhoons uproot trees and buildings, and should someone remark to you, "Nice day, isn't it?" – answer without hesitation, "Isn't it lovely?"

A similar principle emerges when you are talking about politics. Let's talk politics.

Politics

My friend Sandy ran into his ex-colleague, Barry, in downtown Detroit. They had worked together on multiple projects for a large company.

Barry, "Hey, Sandy. How are you?"

Sandy, "I am doing well. I like the entrepreneurial life. How about you?"

Barry, "I am retired but busier than ever. I am organizing the previous mayor Ned's re-election campaign. He finished his jail term last week."

Sandy, "I am glad you are enjoying public service."

Barry, "Well, it is time to give back. Ned has paid his dues. He is a Democrat. He has my support."

Sandy, "Good luck with your campaign. I have to run to a meeting. Let us catch up sometime. Call me."

Barry, "I sure will."

There is a profound American saying, "Friends who want to stay friends don't discuss religion or politics." It implies a classic technique in making friends selectively. If you want to maintain an amicable relationship, do not contradict when discussing politics. Either agree or politely deflect the conversation. On the other hand, if you are not too crazy about the other person, take a diagonally opposing view no matter how you truly feel about the issue.

The fundamental concept of American politics is the two-party system. The essence of the two-party system is that there are always only two political positions on any and every issue. Under no circumstances, can a member of a party have an opinion different from the official stance of the party. In that sense, the two political parties behave like two herds of sheep.

Sandy later explained to me, "Barry is a good man and a staunch Democrat. I am a Republican. I do not discuss politics with him. There is no need to lose a friend."

In many other free countries, politics is all that people talk about. If you are an immigrant, citizen or not, from one of those countries, here is some advice for you. Stay out of politics. Internalize and understand American values first.

American culture has a deeply rooted an indisputable reality. Americans respect and zealously protect their freedoms at all levels, from freedom of speech to protecting animal rights. Let me elaborate.

Freedom

Freedom of speech

"You may speak or write whatever you like" is quite straightforward, or is it? It is complicated if we cannot agree upon the definition of "speech." Just as yoga stretches test the contortion abilities of the human body, constitution lawyers continue to test the limits of the meaning of a simple word, "speech." For example, a corporate entity can contribute an unlimited amount of funds to a political party. Freedom of speech protects it. Did you disrespect the national flag? No problem. Freedom of speech protects it.

One way or other, most actions Americans want to take are related to the civil liberties that they zealously protect. The fundamental rights and freedoms are enshrined in the American constitution. Here are a few observations on the new interpretations of these rights and liberties.

The freedom of bicycling

Americans in auto vehicles are willing, up to a point, to obey traffic signals, but the very idea that an American bicyclist should follow the same traffic rules is outrageous. An American's right to bicycle right into a moving vehicle is secure and so is his reason to bicycle at night without light or flashers. Americans are not the people to squander such valuable liberties.

The right to refuse a breath test

Americans defend this essential right passionately. Most argue against the examination by saying that on an average day, they do not exceed four whiskeys, three beers, and maybe five glasses of wine. The Mothers Against Drunk Driving (MADD) organization, trying to deprive Americans of their right to kill on the road, is far worse than a tyrant is. It is a killjoy.

The right to animal-cross

Animal crossings have produced a different mindset in a large number of Americans. Its origin may have been in India where cows, dogs, sheep, horses, donkeys wander around on the streets freely. Just like humans, animals have a right to move around safely. The fact that we have paved the streets and roads for auto vehicle traffic should not diminish their freedom to move around, or at least be able to cross the road safely.

It all began with deer, moose in some areas, causing significant damage to the auto vehicles in a clash. Thanks to the strategic minds of animal rights lovers, we now have animal crossing signs everywhere. As soon as an animal sets foot on the road, the vehicle must come to a complete halt. Anything less than that is a motor vehicle driving violation.

I have recently heard that the traffic authorities are considering adding animals to the list. Possible candidates are raccoons, squirrels, rabbits, skunks, and porcupines. It is estimated that a high number of road kills are wild turkeys. The traffic authorities are reluctant to include wild turkey to the animal crossing list as many find this the best way of getting a bird for Thanksgiving.

Another discussion topic unique to the USA is how best to lead the world. Why is this important to Americans?

Leading the World

In the early seventies, when I first came to the U.S., the Vietnam War had ended. The Cuban crisis, Nazism, Fascism, etc. were history. The U.S. was the clear economic and military leader of the world.

Then, Germany, China, and Japan industrialized and grew their economies at a rapid pace. The BRIC countries, Brazil, Russia, India, and China, followed by high growth. Instead of continually importing goods and services, they betrayed and began exporting to the U.S. What is the U.S. supposed to manufacture and export? Arms and ammunition? Long live the NRA.

To maintain leadership, what is the best economic model for the U.S.? According to one uncorroborated research study, about 5% of Americans are for capitalism, 4% against it, 3% support capitalism with social programs, and the rest don't know. They are simply confused about the whole issue.

Fortunately, some self-proclaimed scholars claim to know the answer. To propagate their find, they have written books on how to maintain world leadership. Their books remain mostly unnoticed. They just do not know how to market themselves or their books.

Lecturing their ideas to associations, forming clubs to spread their theory, or holding public meetings at the steps of Capitol Hill will not make any difference. No one will blink an eye. Instead, if they were to, with a few of their supporters, take a knee facing the flag on Capitol Hill, they would be the top story on the Internet. If they were to do this nude, the pictures would be hypnotic, and they would dominate the media for almost the whole week.

Here are some marketing concepts explained with hypothetical examples for the immigrant scholars to emulate (these concepts may also work in Great Britain and its largest ex-colony, India).

Let us say you have finally figured out the mix of qigong exercises, herb-rich diet, meditation, and the breathing techniques that Li Ching-Yuen used to live a 256 years long healthy life. This could benefit humanity a great deal and be disastrous for the drug companies, qualifying you for the Nobel Prize for killing two birds with one stone.

If you attempt to publish your discovery in medical journals or take it to relevant institutions, nothing significant will happen. A small group of academic professionals may read it and pat you on your back. On the other hand, if you grow a long beard, wrap a "Swami" turban, wear no clothes except to cover private parts, sit cross-legged on top of a mound in Central Park in New York City, periodically dance on one leg, and go on an indefinite fast, thousands will come out to cheer you. People will take special breaks to show respect for you, and traffic around the park will be jammed. You will draw national (or even global) attention. You will be a sought out coach. Everyone will want your opinion and advice on varied topics except on the subject of living longer.

Some believe that America is not the innovation leader anymore (I am not one of them—just for the record). Do you remember the days of operator-assisted telephone calls made on corded phones? How about waiting for weeks for someone to type and distribute your two-page report? Or, when you bought a whole lot of stamps, envelopes and writing paper to communicate with your family and friends? Well, America invented the Internet and smartphones to replace all that. America is still an innovation leader.

If you, as an immigrant with a strategic perspective, do not agree and want people to listen to your alternative thoughts, then go to other people's gatherings, make obnoxious signs, and scream and yell at somebody prominent (anybody). If that does not convince the world that your thoughts and opinions about the U.S. leadership are worth paying attention to, nothing will.

If you are one of the scholars, who are unhappy selling two books over two years and living on a total yearly income of $5, going forward, your action plan is apparent. Begin smoking tobacco in an Einstein style pipe, shave your head or grow shoulder length hair, and advertise that you write books on world leadership as recommended by animals, especially pets. Start selling your books wrapped in pet blankets. Make alliances with pet companies and sell your books attached to litterbags. Hold exclusive sales of these bundled products at pet shows. Most likely, your future will be set. Your books will be in such a demand that you may have to have the printer install another production line. You will make millions and reach celebrity status as the "Animal Envoy with a Pipe."

Americans are serious about their world leadership responsibility. However, they also know how to live their life to the fullest and therefore, have many passions.

The American Passion

Food

Mike and I walked into a restaurant for dinner in Haarlem, the Netherlands. There was a short waiting line, the serving portions were small, and the ambiance was excellent.

Eating is the number one national passion for an otherwise detached American population. The Americans are rather candid about it and admit that they love all kinds of food. Where else can you find every type of ethnic food that the world knows?

Some of the most watched TV programs in the U.S. tell people how to cook and what to eat. The cook and diet books frequently are the best sellers on the favorite media lists. Armed with vast food insight, Americans crowd an infinite number of restaurants in the U.S.

Americans use apps to catch up on the ratings of eateries in numerous categories and verify the reviews in their extensive discussions at social get-togethers. Even when they do not have plans to go out to eat, they talk about food or stream the latest dining specials just for fun, and then go out to eat and have the time of their life.

Mike and I finished dinner at our usual pace and looked around. Most guests were still there. The Dutch have this infuriating habit of chewing a lot longer. They are in no hurry and claim to taste the meal. Americans are busy, doing something. They will devour three times the food in that much time. We did order more food and gulped it down. The lazy Dutch were still chewing!

The number two American passion is sports.

Sports and Soul

I invited, Yeshe, the son of a Tibetan friend, to join me and my friend, Jerry, on Thanksgiving Day at my house. Two bitter rival NFL teams, the Falcons and Saints, were a close matchup in the Thanksgiving game.

Yeshe is an analyst at a prominent financial firm in New York City. He is also a "new" immigrant. Jerry was curious about how Yeshe spent his time when not working. Sipping a Macallan scotch, Jerry asked,

"Yeshe, what do you do when you are not working?"
Yeshe, "I meditate. I often ask myself, who am I?"

I saw Jerry smile with sympathy.

Immigrants will meditate regularly, pretend to have strengthened control of their minds with no particular validation, always smile, project confidence, and prefer solitude. This is the soul.

The Asian kind is the most ostentatious soul. Those inflicted with it are usually deep thinkers.

Yeshe continued, "When I leave this bag of flesh and bones, will I come back as animate or inanimate? Goat? Mountain? I often think about this complex puzzle and wonder what karma will get me back as a human. But do I want to come back? Maybe, Nirvana—liberation from the endless cycle of birth and death—is the preferred outcome."

All this is very deep—and the soul, nothing else.

The American soul focuses on sports instead.

America has by far the most prominent sports industry in the world. If you want to be genuinely American, you must learn to enjoy sports, which is distinctly American. All real Americans play baseball, football, golf, and many other games. A famous American president called baseball a wartime morale booster.

During WWII, soldiers used baseball lingo and facts when confronting suspected enemy infiltrators attempting to pass themselves off as allies. There were service members' teams across all theaters of war, and baseball was being played recreationally whenever ball diamonds could be carved out.

There was even some bewilderment among some of the allied soldiers because they considered the passion of American soldiers playing baseball in the war zones slightly immature.

Then there are American football and golf. Ignorant immigrants cannot reconcile the fact that players carrying a ball in their hands are actually playing football. They are puzzled to see otherwise perfectly healthy adults excited and aspirational about driving a tiny ball into a small hole.

Immigrants, especially from Asia, are also confused about the third passion of Americans, "Romance."

Romance

If the South Asian youth wants to declare his love to a girl, he kneels down, kisses her hand, talks silly, and tells her that she is the most attractive, charming and beautiful woman in the world. He says to her that she has something in her, something special that only a few million other women have and he would be willing to give his life for her. This is a standard, everyday speech of love in Asian countries.

Americans are a lot more practical about romance. Their presence is all about interests and passions.

In America, the young man smiles and looks into his girl's eyes and reveals that he is into paddle boarding and loves watching baseball. He follows that with a proposal, "I say...what about..." If the girl likes his company and finds him at least attractive, she will say something to the effect, "I never tried paddle boarding, but would love to watch a baseball game together."

This happens on the first date and is kind of the norm. If they actually enjoy similar activities and have common interests, the dating will continue. They make a concerted effort to know each other.

An immigrant should follow the same guidelines. I have seen immigrants trying to be the twinkle of somebody's eye and the heartthrob without paying much attention to common areas of interest. Most of the time, that does not work.

Here is a typical dialog between an Asian immigrant and an American date.

Immigrant, "Will you go out with me?"
Date, "No."
Immigrant, "Why not?"
Date, "Because."
Immigrant, "Because of what?"
Date, "Because."

All men, especially immigrants, need to share information and then listen to her attentively. Most immigrants are trying too hard to show how good they are, and not paying attention to what she is saying or how she is responding.

An enticing meal followed by watching a film is another favorite dating activity. Oh! Talking about movies...

Movies

In the early 1970s, somewhere in southern California, a bearded young man had a dream of turning old samurai films, Eastern philosophies, and something like Flash Gordon into an operatic adventure set in space. The original "Star Wars" was born. The film is the third-highest-grossing film of all time, raking in close to $2 billion when adjusted for inflation.

After the massive success of "Star Wars" in 1977, the Hollywood producers had an epiphany. They recognized that the majority of the American public is not dull and boring and that a fast-moving sci-fi built on popular mythologies and future technologies is not bound to fail. It was a big leap of faith to make movies on such a premise, but it has proved worthy.

Then there is the ethnic movie where a young man of Mumbai wins the Indian version of "Who Wants to Be a Millionaire." Accused of cheating, the young man recounts his life story to the police, illustrating how he can answer each question correctly. The movie, "Slumdog Millionaire," had a general release in the U.S. on January 23, 2009. The $15 million budget film won eight academy awards including Best Film, five Critics' Choice awards, and four Golden Globes.

Let the examples above not mislead you to believe that you can make great movies with a low budget and without hiring prominent actors. The success of "Star Wars," built on a modest budget, was a fluke. A samurai could not possibly have had any acting skills. The ethnic movie was successful because its content was customized to present what the Americans want to hear even if it was a blatant misrepresentation.

If you, as an immigrant, want to make a Hollywood caliber movie, your first objective should be to dispel the belief that you can make a great movie without an exorbitant budget. Second, to be successful in the U.S., you must reinforce the "American impression of the others" even if it is false.

I present a few newer trends that you must also recognize.

1. The rumor that Americans love technology because they are lazy is utterly false. The misleading perception is because many films show robots doing household work, exponential growth in online shopping and home delivery, and in self-driving

vehicles. Americans are passionate about technology and sci-fi. It is, therefore, essential that some technical advancement, real or imaginary, show up in your film and mesmerize the audience with its impact on their lives.

2. The technological advances have made more time available for personal development and self-improvement activities. Increasingly, Americans are practicing meditation, yoga, silence, and solitude. They prefer succinct communication to preserve their energy. Therefore, the words and phrases such as "crap" and "dammit" have become trendy for pithy expression. As a movie producer, you must collect a complete list of such words and phrases. Use them in your film. It will make the movie remarkably more realistic.

3. For a movie to succeed, customization to suit the American taste is almost mandatory. I have heard that a producer had a "Taj Mahal" built in the studio. When his team went to India for filming the movie, he carried his own "Taj Mahal" to the small town named Agra where the real Taj Mahal is located. Amazingly, he was right. The original monument is too old and is suitable for Indians—who are foreigners anyway—but

not up to the standard for a Hollywood production.

4. Americans love past events filmed as satirical comedies. For example, "Inglorious Basterds" featuring Brad Pitt and Elizabeth Taylor portraying Cleopatra as a lovely woman were box office hits. Therefore, I conclude that with a slight change in a subject's persona, you can make outstanding films. I recommend that you consider remaking "Godfather" as a romantic comedy, and "Wikipedia" as a spiritual musical.

America is the largest market for everything. The marketers have done a commendable job to get the American consumer addicted to shopping.

Shopping

Yup! Shopping is also one of the top passions of Americans. The minimalists can make all the noise they want, Americans just love to shop. How they buy is constantly changing though.

I am glad that there was no Internet in the seventies. There were no smartphones, either. People went to glamorous malls for shopping and more. It was a social event. These malls helped me in turning myself into a real American. I learned the arts of window-shopping and socializing with complete strangers.

Now, hardly anyone goes to the grand shopping malls of the seventies and eighties. Most in-person socializing is at the grocery stores. I should have seen it coming. This trend is in harmony with American passion for food, and the constant pursuit of greater efficiency. You buy your groceries, meet new people, and if you like someone, have a drink or meal at the eatery, available at most grocery stores. This is American ingenuity—converting a chore into a fun social event. Most people do it regularly, about once a week.□

Travel

Vacation

The American concept of vacation is taking weekend trips to the Poconos (if you are living in the tristate area—New York, New Jersey, Pennsylvania). Those residing in the northeast prefer weekend breaks to Cape Cod or Martha's Vineyard. Americans in the northwest go skiing, visit Yellowstone Park, gamble in Las Vegas or Reno, take a stroll on Hollywood Boulevard and slide back into their igloo as soon as old man winter returns. The residents of the north Midwest come out of their shelters in late spring and summer. After a long, typically miserable winter, they enjoy mowing their lawns. People in the Southeast states live in what they call paradise. There is no need to go anywhere except short trips to the shooting range or local watering hole for fishing. No one pays attention to what people living in the southern Midwest and southwest do for time off.

Senior Americans love vacationing on a Caribbean cruise. This has many advantages. Lodging, boarding, and meals are economical and included in the total package price paid upfront. The number of meals and amount of food are organized to suit the American preference—a large quantity of low-quality food.

In winter, Florida is a popular destination. Families go to Orlando. Teenagers and young adults crowd the beaches in Clearwater, Fort Lauderdale, Miami, and West Palm. The middle-aged prefer Sarasota (rumor is that the town does have a life).

Why do Americans travel?

A straightforward explanation is that they all want to be in a warmer place. It is not a complete answer. Another important driver is the love of photographs and videos of themselves.

Scantily dressed, families take pictures everywhere in Disney World and Universal Studios. The young adults and teenagers click cameras on the beaches where they do not see a need to wear anything more than the minimum required by law. The middle-aged and seniors, whose skin needs ironing, do clothe well. Then they all post photos and videos all over social media.

Caution. Travelers to Florida may want to buy an artificial intelligence based interpreting machine. Oh! It looks like regular earbuds with a built-in microphone except that you speak and hear in English while the local Floridian speaks and understands in Spanish.

When it comes to travel, Millennials are smart. They will select the least expensive travel destination served by one or more no-frills airlines.

The auto vehicle is the number one mode of travel in the United States. Driving in the U.S., in many ways, is about the same as anywhere else. A car breaking down in the snow and wind gives about the same pleasure outside New York City as outside Sao Paulo.

So, what is different?

Driving, Drivers, And Cops

After graduating, I dumped everything I owned into my 1972 Buick LeSabre and headed towards New Jersey. Driving on Route 70 just past Indianapolis, I was pulled over by a cop. I rolled down my window, put on a huge smile and was looking at the twin brother of Archie Bunker, except this guy was a police officer.

There are some timeless pointers which an immigrant driver must keep in mind.

1.   In American towns, the driving speed limit changes without notice. The police are eagerly waiting to catch the speeding drivers. The cops' desire for exceeding "ticket quota" does not create a conflict of interest.

2.   Many new immigrants complain that it is practically impossible to spot a cop car checking the traffic speeds. I present here a few clues, which may assist immigrants with keen observing ability.
   • The police always use a full-size, wide-body, American car.
   • The car is generally white or black but could be any color.
   • At least one uniformed police officer is sitting in it.

• The word, POLICE, is written in large capital letters on the front, rear, and sides of the car. The letters light up in the dark.
• Usually, there are "red, orange and blue" lights attached conspicuously on the car roof.

The police officer looked at my brown face, bent forward and pointing at the speedometer, said, "65. No more than 65. Okay?" He was also very kind to use sign language—showing six fingers and then five fingers—making sure I understood what he was saying. I nodded—but, didn't say a word—and he signaled me to drive off.

At a truck stop a few miles further on the highway, I was chatting with the bartender while sipping on a chilled beer when I felt a slightly heavy hand on my shoulder.

"I thought you did not know English!" The Archie Bunker look-alike cop was staring at me.
"Sir, you assumed that. I had no reason to speak. Can I buy you a beer?"

He smiled, then laughed. We shook hands. He refused my offer to buy him a beer but did sit down with me for small talk.

Sitting alone in their parked car hidden behind bushes or some other visibility barrier, cops begin to feel lonely. Therefore, they just might stop you for some reason or no apparent reason. Maybe, they just want to chat and learn something about you. It's possible.

In 1978, I was driving through 600 blocks of the historic district in Mobile, Alabama. Mesmerized with the beautiful canopy of live oak trees with their snaking branches covered with resurrection fern, I completely missed the traffic light changing from red to orange to green and back to red. Slowly a cop car rolled up next to my stopped vehicle.

"Where are you from, son?" a middle-aged cop with a slight beer belly asked.

"Well, sir. I work for AT&T in New York City. I am here to visit our district sales office."

"Oh! You are from a big city. And, that is also a rich city."

"Yes, sir," beaming with joy that someone recognized the importance of being a New Yorker.

The officer bent forward a little and with a smirk on his face said, "Well son, we are a small town and not New York City rich. Our traffic lights have only three colors. We can afford 'three-color' traffic lights only. You move when it turns green next time!"

After the deregulation in 1978, the air travel prices nose-dived, and so did the quality of service and onboard amenities. However, the number of people traveling by airplanes increased many folds. American airline companies are ingenious. They have found several friendly ways to make the travel enjoyable.

Ingenious Airlines

Alyssa loves her job with an airline company at one of the busiest airports in the country. She has a customer facing position, and she enjoys playing "Catch Me If You Can" games with the obedient travelers. She explained her four most favorite games.

Fake Forecast

Announce "possible delay" when most travelers are already in the waiting lounge. Blame the weather. The fact that it is calm and sunny outside is irrelevant. Some factors are unseen.

When many travelers have wandered off to a coffee shop or a restaurant, have a recent immigrant make an unintelligible "now boarding" announcement. It is fun to watch travelers, who have understood only two words, "now boarding," hustle back.

Hurry-Up and wait

Once all travelers are on board, announce a possible delay due to a necessary "technical" matter. It will probably take no more than twenty minutes after the engineer begins to work at it. It is amusing to observe the facial expressions of travelers with connecting flights.

Toilet tantrum

While in the air, regiment access to the toilets by the passengers. Reasons for doing so are several—plane ascending, plane descending, turbulence, non-serving refreshments cart in the aisle, waiting-line regulation (if there is none, manufacture one), etc., etc. It is hilarious to watch the passengers, who need to use the toilet, squirm in their seats.

Comedy as a career

You can practice your stand-up comedian skills for a captive audience. The applause or lack of it will guide you on whether to pursue stand-up comedy as a full-time career.

No big need to learn beforehand, how to get around in your destination city or town. They are all well-planned and have friendly people.

American Cities and Towns

Americans are exceptionally organized people. This is noticeable in the American way of building cities and towns.

The Manhattan borough of New York City is a grid of avenues running vertical (north and south), and streets running horizontal (east and west). Most roads permit only one-way driving. This is effective in maximizing the revenue for the taxi operators.

In Manhattan, there are certain locales dedicated to a specific commercial community. Advertising agencies are on Madison Avenue, Broadway theaters are in midtown Manhattan, the diamond district is on 47th street, garment district is on 39th and 40th streets, the financial community is on Wall Street, etc. This is a strategic component of planning, and if you become a city planner, you can build upon this idea. Locate all grocery stores at the Upper East Side on First or Second Avenue and put all men's conveniences all along Broadway.

The majority of U.S. cities do not follow any specific pattern. In NJ, for example, all cities and towns are mostly lumps of residential and commercial developments set randomly across the state. Doctors, lawyers, financial brokers, insurance agents—as examples—are available all over, so you can call on a good or at least an expensive professional in any area.

An American city is a broad conspiracy to confuse new immigrants. The "Best Practices" section of the city planning manual usually signals the intent.

1. In NYC, the streets are always straight. New York City residents are not paranoid about privacy and love to see one end of the road from the other end. In San Francisco, streets are mostly S-shaped. Chicago roads are circular loops.

2. There is a certain level of camouflaging of the numbering of the houses. It is not necessary. to put even numbers on one side, odd numbers on the other, and begin numbering from the south or east. In many towns, there is no numbering displayed. People are particular about their privacy.

    In Princeton, NJ, there is numbering in hidden alleys connected to the main street. Of course, the main street itself has no need to post any numbers.

3. Whenever a road bends or does not turn but only crosses a traffic light, its name changes. However, if there is a big break in the street due to a park or office complex—that actually makes it two different streets—the name stays the same. If, by any chance, a road is straight but too long in somebody's opinion, its name changes after every few miles (Kildee, Brandywine, Sunset, and so on.)

4. Streets are called by various names: street, road, way, lane, avenue, alley, parkway, boulevard, walk, etc.

5. There are streets, parks, squares and roads of the same name in adjacent towns in the same county. It is easier to remember the same names. With several Washington Roads and Broad Streets in the nearby cities, life is less confusing. To further reduce confusion, some planners name towns the same in contiguous counties—Washington Township is a popular choice.

6. The street name signs are painted clearly on narrow panels. To smartly hide the boards, they are set on tall poles. They are placed too high or too low, in shadow and darkness, at a forty-five-degree angle or

better still, not there at all. Just like texting, the signs distract the drivers and therefore are either unobtrusive or missing.

Whether at home or in the destination city, Americans switch on the media to watch the news and of course, the commercials. What do they see?

The Media

News Reporting

On December 19, 2018, the President of the United States tweeted, "We have won against ISIS. Our boys, our young women, our men — they're all coming back, and they're coming back now."

As I recall, here is how the media reported it.

The New York Times

Trump to Withdraw U.S. Forces from Syria, ending the military campaign and ceding a strategically vital country to Russia and Iran.

Bloomberg

Senator Lindsey Graham, the president's golf buddy, tweeted, "pulling out of Syria would be a "boost to ISIS" and a "huge Obama-like mistake."

Los Angeles Times

Trump decides to withdraw from Syria and build a border wall instead.

New York Magazine – Intelligencer

U.S. Troops will eventually leave Syria.

As an immigrant, act ignorant and politely ask some questions, only to be part of the conversation. Here is an example of what not to ask:

- How do we plan to exit?
- How many Americans even knew, over 2,000 soldiers have been on the ground in Syria for years?
- Why are Congress members upset when troops get to come home without their approval, not when we deploy them without debate and proper authorization?
- Why weren't the politicians actually up front to the American people about the high costs of another war?

I recommend that you leave such questions for the U.S. born citizens. However, you are welcome to enjoy the TV commercials. Their credibility is without any question the highest.

Commercials

All commercials, especially those on TV, are metaphorical art. You may think the seller is lying. Not really. The seller is merely magnifying the derived benefit, if any, for better comprehension by simpler minds. The style includes superlatives with daffy implications (smoke this pipe tobacco and you will convert from an ignoramus to a genius).

If you are working as a marketing professional, there is a way to differentiate your advertising. Consider this.

Expensive Auto: Buy this car, and you will attract the opposite gender as honey attracts flies. On the other hand, you may not.
Or,
Slimax: Try the diet of Bhutanese Monks now offered in a pill. Some people lost excess weight. Some lost their lives. You may survive.
Or,
You may try to appeal to the American sense of honesty.

Faux-Cola soft drink. Watch Mr. Mote from Tuscaloosa, Alabama, try the regular Cola and our new Faux-Cola. Mr. Mote, which one would you say tastes better?

Mr. Mote, "This one."

Advertiser, "Thank you for your honesty. That is the regular cola. You do not get to go on a free cruise, not a big deal. Nevertheless, my fellow Americans just drink Faux-Cola. Who wants to drink the same old dark colored, fuzzy, sugary drink anyway? Faux-Cola is the newest.

Or,
Just do not make any exaggerated claims. Be ambiguous, in other words, talk like a politician.

Tampa Draft Beer. It is locally brewed and dirt cheap. Who cares what it tastes like?

Or,
Can you tell the difference between our maple syrup and WD-40? We cannot.

Or,
Coconut-Turmeric cookies are healthy. Just swallow them. You do not need to experience the taste.

The world is catching up to American media dexterity and public personas. Yup! You read it right. The American public personas.

Personas En General

Richness

If you want to help the poor, you must be rich. However, you must not flaunt your wealth. A common notion is to wear casual attire, drive an old model souped-up car, preferably without a muffler, and talk about philanthropy. I do not fully qualify to lay out in details the art of looking and acting rich without showing off. However, I can share some traits I have observed.

The Toys

In the 1970s, to look rich, an Aston Martin One, La Ferrari, or at least a Bentley was a must. A palatial abode to go along with it was highly desirable. Today the nouveau riche immigrants, scam artists, attention seeking television celebrities, and pseudo newscasters buy Bentleys and Aston Martins. The aristocrats buy vintage Corvettes and Camaros, trucks, and bicycles.

Retreats

After I completed a business turnaround in the Midwest, my friend Richard, a retired philanthropist, insisted that I temporarily retreat from the world. As a refuge, he offered his exotic cottage in a wooded area, close to the beach, about sixty miles outside Barnesdale, Oregon.

You must talk about your retreats as exotic destinations. If you can insert casually that such hideouts are calming breaks from your disguised unemployment, you will come across as a person of opulence.

After a one and a half mile long walk in the woods on a narrow dirt path, I finally reached the hideaway. The cottage had no stress-inducing modern amenities, such as TV, heat, air-conditioning, gas or a bed with a mattress. It was the perfect place for solitude, deep meditation, and a scenic walk to Rockaway Beach. Water was available from a small stream nearby.

Connections

The company you keep makes a big difference in projecting your cloaked richness. Unlike Great Britain, America does not have the legendary titles—Lords, Dukes, Earls. However, there are regular sought-after classes of people. These are the oil-rich Arabs, Eastern European models for their sharp and sexy looks, and the Irish for I don't know what.

The new coveted class looks different.
These are the Silicon Valley billionaires, the
hi-tech affluent Asians including ostentatious
Indians, and the wizards shaping the financial
markets.

Pastimes

You may not go on hunting trips, but
you must own a modest collection of guns.
You will be a highly respected aristocrat if you
can talk about various types of firearms, their
peculiar styles and capabilities, and engaging
anecdotal experiences you have had using
them. Proudly share your expertise in cleaning
a dead pheasant.

After a lively discussion of guns, warm
up the kinship with a review of cigars and
wines. For some reason, gun collectors are
also cigar smokers and wine connoisseurs
with a humidor and a cellar as standard
fixtures at their residences.

Winnings

With advances in Internet technologies,
barista and Uber jobs have become trendy.
These jobs generate sufficient cash to buy
lottery tickets. Make no big deal if you win one
of these even if it is for a million dollars or
more. Calmly state that it is not going to
change your life in any way. After all, what do

a million dollars matter if you already have a car, a pad, Internet connection, and a loving partner? Of course, do not even think about giving up your barista job or Uber driving.

Wall Street

A little uncool with the Millennials, the boomers, are still enamored with the economic dynamics on Wall Street. It is essential to know terms, such as calls, puts, alpha, price-earning, etc. to project the image that you have a portfolio of financial instruments. The fundamental concept is to "buy low" and "sell high." Please do not try the other way around—it could adversely affect your mental and physical health.

I do not directly invest in any instrument on Wall Street. I park my money at one of the investment companies. They make over 100 percent profit, give me an annual return of five to six percent, from which I pay them 2 percent as a management fee and of course, there is the income tax. The result is gratifying. I know that my money's value is not eroding.

Ingenious Millennials

Recently I recommended a great book (priced $14.99) to a millennial at Starbucks. She replied with a long face, "I can't afford it."

She then went right back to staring at her latest version of the iPhone.

The millennials face an uphill battle showing their poverty. The problem became acute when Apple raised the price of the iPhone to about one thousand dollars.

All hats off to the millennials, though. Despite their poverty, they drive a shiny car, buy avocados as a staple food, spend hours on a smartphone socializing, and making this world a better place. All this without any job, is a reflection of their great ingenuity.

Considering the tough challenges of the millennials, why are so many people surprised at their support of social programs and the bureaucrats running them? Who are these bureaucrats?

The Bureaucrats

The British invented bureaucracy.
Europe embraced it. The U.S. privatized it.

There is considerable overlap between
the European civil servant and the American
public servant, the bureaucrat. The American
corporate bureaucrat (primarily in large
monopolies and duopolies such as Internet
Service Providers, utilities, banks, insurance
companies, etc.), is different, but striving hard
to emulate the first two.

In Europe, civil servants have built into
their culture a military-like authority. They
consider themselves equivalent to
commanders in armed forces. They cannot
control armies, so they manage the approvals
and permits. They do not lose battles. They
just lose records and documents in the
cyberspace. They are convinced that the sole
purpose of a society is to keep the civil
servants employed.

The European civil servants somehow
shared their expertise with the American
bureaucrats at the local municipal offices. The
bureaucrats converted their acquired skills
into a game, "who gives up first," with wicked

homeowners seeking a permit for home improvement or some silly project like that.

At the municipal offices, a busy looking bureaucrat will send the homeowner to the zoning office on the fifth floor. The zoning office staff will promptly direct the homeowner to another office on the second floor. The team on the second floor cannot believe that the homeowner is there interrupting their routine. They convince the homeowner that his trip to the second floor is misguided. They send him back to the primary office in the basement.

At the primary office in the basement, the knowledgeable staff persuades the dumb homeowner to go to the fifth-floor office again. The authorities on the fifth-floor office send him to the second floor, and the process goes on endlessly until the homeowner gets tired of the whole system. Many homeowners give up in desperation or go crazy and seek admission to the state rehab center, which is run by another set of bureaucrats.

If they do seek admission at the rehab center, the receptionist there promptly sends them to an office on the fifth floor. The office on the fifth floor sends them down to the second-floor office, which guides them back to the receptionist. The relay continues until the homeowners give up being crazy.

Knowledgeable sources tell me that the bureaucrats who know their way around and how to deal with the officials have the highest success rate of gaining admission at the rehab center.

The American bureaucrat, unlike the bully of Europe, serves the American public dutifully. Before the civil rights movement, the Immigration Department would order an illegal alien to leave the country. The ICE (or, its counterpart then), would usually deny the extension of the stay if requested by an illegal alien. He stayed on all the same. After a while, ICE would send him the following notice (This is my imagination gone wild):

Dear illegal alien,

The "Immigration and Customs Enforcement (ICE)" thank you for visiting our country. It is an honor to receive your application for the extension of your illegal stay.
We regret to inform you that you are ineligible for the extension. Please leave this country within 24 hours. If you fail to do so, we will extradite you by force to a land of our

choice via the least cost mode of transportation.

Sincerely,
The Bureaucrat.

A corporate bureaucrat considers himself no military officer but a glorified business executive. He is smooth and courteous and smiles with a superior aura. He is agreeable, obliging, and often clueless.

If so, you may ask, how can he help achieve the mission of his large and socially responsible corporation, namely, frustrate the customers seeking service, to the point where they have no choice but to leave the corporate bureaucrat alone to watch his favorite show on Netflix? There is various customer support, "Best Practices," to secure this mission.

1.   "Frequently Asked Questions (FAQs)" – provide answers to questions that no one is asking.
2.   "Help" – All information reads like legal briefs and is meaningless for the customers.
3.   "Bundling" - Your problems can be solved with "bundling" offers. If you buy this additional product or service your current

non-functioning product or service would be cheaper overall.

4. "Live Chat" - Encourage "live" chat with a human being if a customer can pass the " touch-tone" exercise—press 1 for technical support, press 2 for billing, press 3 for sales, etc., etc. Of course, there is an option for verbal input, which works only if you have a "flat" accent. A British visitor repeated the word "eleven" at least ten times before giving it up.

5. "Caller Comprehension" - Test customers' comprehension ability. The "customer support" person is an Indian, Malaysian, Filipino, or from some other country where you never knew people could speak English.

6. "Safety First" – A corporate bureaucrat never makes decisions. He trains his staff to follow a similar safe practice. Safety is first. The customer support person, having understood the issue, only 'promises to answer' – 'likely answer,' – or –– 'research' caller's question.

7. "24 x 7 Availability" - In theory, a corporate bureaucrat is present always to serve the customers. In practice, he is either on a conference call or on a lunch break, or in but having his coffee, or just unavailable.

In Europe, influential people, or those who have friends, relatives, business associates, etc., in an office may have their requests fulfilled. In America, there is no such corruption, and the public servant or the corporate bureaucrat will not give a damn who you are and whom you know. This is the real magnificence of democracy.

Not all bureaucrats are ordinary. Some are Ivy League scholars. How can you tell? Read on.

An Ivy League Scholar

The Ivy League scholars talk down uniformity and go the extra mile to stick with the ivy style, which unknown to immigrants, is actually a style of its own.

Ivy style is more elegant and dressed up than the casual undertones of the American culture. Typical casual is appropriate for garden parties, sailing, and casual affairs. Ivy style is for more formal, casual occasions such as attending class at Harvard Law, going on a dinner date or an event your parents insisted you participate with them at the golf club after ordering you to leave the boat shoes at home.

The ivy style separates the men of Harvard, Princeton, and Yale from the youth at other colleges. The ivy style is a way to recognize instantly, a member of your social class. One thing to keep in mind is representing yourself through your wardrobe as a member of one of the elite universities or colleges in the world.

The Ivy League scholar will wear penny loafers and will wear shoes without socks only in the heat of summer. An Ivy League scholar – while he loves a sports jacket – will wear a suit almost half of the time. A typical youth from other colleges will rarely wear a suit and usually opt for a navy sports jacket instead.

When it comes to standard American attire, it is about convenience, comfort, and style. For the Ivy League scholar, it is about style followed by comfort and then convenience.

A typical young man will throw on the first polo shirt he finds in his closet and pairs it with go-to-hell pants (any boldly colored pair of trousers, with or without a pattern or motif including designs like madras or pink seersucker). An Ivy League scholar will pair it with a sleeveless sweater and wear beige linen pants.

When it comes to sports, typical youth and ivy styles connect well. Golf and tennis remain the favorites. Weekends in Southampton are still an inspiring way to spend the summer. There is nothing better than spending an afternoon sipping G&Ts on a sailboat during winters in Palm Beach.

One of my Harvard graduate immigrant friends used to add HBS (Harvard Business School) after his last name. In the mid-1970s, he met a lively woman at a barbeque gathering on my boat in Sandy Hook, NJ. Later, he asked me to find out what she thought of him. Here is how the conversation went with the then young woman.

"Hey, Judy. What do you think about my friend Edwardo? He likes you."

"Oh, well. Edwardo is handsome and a likable man. But he is too much Ivy League!"

"He did go to Harvard. Why do you say that?"

"He introduced himself as Edwardo C, HBS!"

Judy and Edwardo are married and live in Key West, Florida. I met them again. Now she calls him too 'preppy!' As an Ivy League scholar, Edwardo recognizes that the clothing is still the same; the distinction depends upon how women refer to the attire —and the men who wear them.

It is essential that the Ivy League scholar always have some facial hair. Shaving and leaving no facial hair is not cool. The Ivy League scholars view complete shaving as an undesirable middle-class trait. (The scholars from Princeton hold the same view about bathing too.)

A little bit of snobbery is necessary because Ivy League scholars have to prove

24x7 that the thoughts of ordinary people on the current issues are too simplistic and not worth their time. Sometimes they feel the same way about the prevailing customs of society. The Ivy League college does an excellent job in helping them give up silly habits—to say, "Hullo," "Thank you," or similar expressions—acquired at home or in school. After spending one semester at an Ivy League, you will not have the slightest remorse trashing an essay written by a high school student in the local newspaper.

Ivy League scholars express their technical views cautiously. They make dramatic statements. "There have been three real scientists in the U.S., J. Robert Oppenheimer, Thomas Edison, and Alexander Graham Bell. The rest of them were either not born here or did not do that great a work." Of course, the Ivy League scholars will include, as the other outstanding scientists, whose scientific work is so irrelevant that the majority of the scientists refuse to recognize it. As to their own scientific discoveries, they lie somewhere in a draft form.

It is essential that the Ivy League scholars publish a few critical reviews, disproving and challenging everybody and everything. They do so with high confidence, quoting Albert Einstein and anything in a foreign language (mostly French or Greek). They let the audience sense what they would be able to do if everyone only listened to them.

A little advice. It is relatively easy to have a few critical reviews published on social media. It costs nothing. However, you must not let others label your review as unfair out of professional envy. Instead, position it as your dedication to a "cause." There are many "causes" floating around. Pick one or invent a new one. The content is not that important as long as the review is critical. I am aware of at least one Ivy League scholar who consistently expresses opinions on significant scientific work backing up the climate change phenomenon. His comments quite clearly indicate that he does not understand an iota of scientific research. Yet, his opinions are having a chillingly high impact on the nation's environmental policies.

Politically, Ivy League scholars are usually to the left. In reality, they are solely for themselves—whatever works to enhance their career is the best.

If you are about to graduate from an Ivy League college, then you must keep a few things in mind:

1. You must not care about the welfare of the masses anywhere in the world. That would be "practical politics." You should be an Ivy League scholar and be interested only in the concerned ideologies.
2. Position yourself as an "outsider" or an "independent." Do not join any party because then you would be "branded?" Whatever the parties claim, it is more exciting to criticize than to be a part of the herd.
3. Do not hesitate to ridicule Russia and China as reactionary and imperialistic, the British Labor party as a gathering of elderly union members, the French Socialists as entitled, the other Western Societies as bourgeois groups, the American labor as slaves of big business, and call all Republicans crypto-fascists.

Invent some of your own unique models and theories, such as:

Only Buddhism can save the world.

Meditation and spirituality are growing immensely in importance, and a possible, working coalition between zombies and neocons would be highly desirable.

The enormous tax breaks to the rich, wealthy, and large corporations would make the populace ultra-rich. Then you can collect a lot more in taxes.

One last thought. Remember the main message here. Always be unique. It is easier than you think; you just need to imitate the habits and maxims of a few thousand other Ivy League scholars.

In some social circles, there is a perception that the Ivy League scholars are natural Don Juans. Maybe. Maybe not. I can only describe my impression of an American Don Juan.

American Don Juan

A typical American Don Juan believes that to be successful, you need to experience failure. This concept is getting exceptional traction. I have failed in attracting the female species every time I have tried. Therefore, now, I must be on the verge of enormous success.

Don Juan believes that the whole purpose of life is to have a great time, go to chic places, and meet charming people. To have a great time means to have a sufficient number of drinks requiring you to call Uber for transportation to wherever you want to go. Chic places are the restaurants in fancy hotels or restaurants with unique theme ambiance, out-of-the-way private clubs, nightclubs and private houses with paintings by famous, albeit dead, artists, an impressive wine cellar and a humidor carrying expensive cigars. Charming people are those who say meaningless things in proper English, and offensive people are those who drop double-entendres in the local jargon.

During the greedy Baby Boomers' era, the man who had little or no money could not be a Don Juan. The Millennials belong to a progressive era, and the mindset is different.

Now the mark of a ladies-man is that irrespective of his financial health he still refuses to do meaningful work.

An American Don Juan approaches an attractive woman with easy-going confidence allowing his natural and unique charisma to come through. He is kind, but not too friendly. He always laughs at other people's jokes but is smart enough to tell a joke from a veiled message. He smiles, but not so much. He doesn't want to come across as a soft, happy-go-lucky, naïve man who needs to get some guts. He is polite in a teasing, blasé manner and grins at everything he does not understand.

He flirts whenever he can. To flirt appropriately, he is witty. "If you had to choose between Leonardo DiCaprio and me, how quickly would you choose me?" He will flirt with anybody's girlfriend or wife but does not forget the possible consequences of illegitimate friendships (unless he has an excellent opportunity, which would be such a pity to miss.).

He makes women laugh. A sense of humor is attractive because being humorous requires intelligence. A self-deprecating type of fun is even better because it also shows high confidence. He does not mean it, and women do not believe it.

He would dress to impress—well-pressed trousers, carefully knotted ties, and silk shirts are the greatest of human values. His shoes match his choice of attire. He adds accessories, like a watch, pocket square, or tie clip, to draw extra attention.

At bars, he tips well and never is sober after 7 p.m.

Are Ivy League scholars and Don Juans the ruling class?

The Rulers and The Ruled

In the satirical novella, Animal Farm (1945) by George Orwell, one of the seven commandments for the pigs is, "All animals are equal, but some animals are more equal than others." Politicians of today want us to tacitly accept that these "more equal than others," are the corporate elite and ultra-rich people. They are the "rulers." They rule the masses with a firm hand and a Mona Lisa smile. The populace that still wants to live the American dream is the "ruled."

There are the traditional corporate elite, ultra-rich people, and a new breed—Ivy League and brand name college-trained financial whizzes —at investment houses and hedge funds populating the corporate boards as directors. The brilliant immigrants, the cream of the crop that America attracts from all over the world do not dream of becoming doctors, engineers, or scientists anymore. Now they aspire to specialize in financial sorcery and be the ruling class.

If you are reading here, you have shown extraordinary patience. It is time to recognize some American idiosyncrasies.

Idiosyncrasies

Sports

In October of every year, you may be tempted to buy tickets to watch the World Series Baseball Championship. Aside from two Canadian teams and one Japanese team, the U.S. is the only major country that plays baseball.

American football? Yes, it is unique to the U.S. too. It has nothing in common with the sport the rest of the world knows as football.

Thumbs Up

Do not be offended if you see someone giving a "thumbs up." It is an affirming gesture. No. It is not akin to raising your middle finger in regions like Australia, India, and the Middle East. These countries need to catch up.

Toilets

An immigrant in the U.S. needs to get comfortable with the American-style public toilet stalls. The fact that there is so much space underneath and around stall doors does not make American public toilets too public. In Britain, the top three things people complain about are, the weather, American toilets, and the weather.

Measures

You may want to change your habits for the order of a few things. For example, when it comes to something as simple as writing the date, Americans typically write as "MM-DD-YY," but the rest of the world writes it as "DD-MM-YY." The voltage requirement for appliances in the U.S. is 110 volts to 115 volts—the rest of the world it is 220 volts. The U.S. is also one of only three countries to follow the imperial measurement system, FPS (Foot, Pound, Second). The other two nations are Myanmar and Liberia.

Flag

The American flag density per square mile is the highest in the world. People in other countries just do not go around decked in the flag of their country.

World Knowledge

I have met numerous self-proclaimed worldly Americans. Most of them have never stepped outside the U.S. For a nation that has a military presence in 177 countries, one would think that Americans would be especially aware of the broader international community. The reality is quite the opposite.

No matter all of the above, you can still live the proverbial "American Dream."

The American Dream

Living the American Dream

How to live the American Dream? Just as a picture conveys a thousand words, an example illustrates things better than pages of theoretical discussion.

Last year, I had arranged a reunion of a few of my college friends at a Tiki Bar and Beach Lounge. We were lazing around sipping beer, when a late year Porsche 911 rolled into the parking lot, about fifty yards away. My friend, Rafael, stepped out with fancy shades and Versace beachwear. I waved at him and asked how he was doing.

"Oh. Living the American Dream," said Rafael as he removed his shirt to expose 240 pounds of blubber and an elegant gold necklace.

A few minutes later, Sam pulled up in his jalopy, a 1980 Corolla. I was delighted to see him. "Hey! Sam. How the hell are you?" Sam waved and with a big smile, answered, "Oh, Living the American Dream."

The American Dream is "the opportunity to define oneself as one chooses."

The American Dream is alive and kicking in the U.S., Australia, Canada, India, and the United Kingdom.

Naturalization

Get Naturalized

For long-time immigrants, it may be time to become an American citizen. Just do it.

There is a path to becoming a citizen of the United States of America. The Americans call the process "naturalization."

I have often wondered at the selection of the term "naturalization." Was I not "natural' before I became an American citizen? Maybe, my command of American English language needs improvement. So, I googled the word "natural."

The search engine spits out the definition of the word natural by several dictionaries, the Thesaurus, and the Wiktionary. Natural is what existed and evolved within the confines of an ecosystem. It is of or relating to nature, without artificial ingredients. It is as expected, or reasonable. For example, music produced by natural organs, such as those of the human throat, in distinction from instrumental music. No process has altered it, and it is free from any intent to deceive or impress others.

With engineering training, I began an investigation of how I materialized. The surviving elderly relatives assured me that my parents did not seek any outside help and did it all by themselves. Is it possible that I was cultivated on a farm and grew up like a plant? If so, I would still result from a natural phenomenon.

I did not feel any urgent need to become a U.S. citizen. However, my employer felt otherwise. To receive clearance from the National Security Agency (NSA) for making technical presentations, I needed to be a proven natural human being with the smarts of an American citizen.

Passing the test and receiving the certificate of citizenship (naturalization) is a piece of cake. Once recognized as a natural person, becoming an American is even simpler. All it requires is to give up your conscience. Just pretend that you are everything you are not, and look down upon everything you are. Always maintain that the American way of doing, whatever it may be, is the best and unmatched.

A few of my Indian-American acquaintances have the correct attitude. As a new immigrant or aspiring to be one, it will behoove you to copy their approach. They are staunch Republicans when they are not Democrats. They are engineers, doctors, traders, builders, hoteliers, restaurant owners, professors, IT experts, and anything that does not entail physical labor.

Indian Americans exhibit deep respect for all Americans—English, French, African, Hispanic, Canadian, Polish, Irish, Italians, Jews, rich, needy, liberals, progressives, conservatives, religious, agnostic and atheists. However, they look down upon Indians who have an accent—every Indian thinks that the other Indian has an inflection—because that is not very American.

Once the U.S. government recognizes you as a "natural" being and accepts you as a citizen, I highly recommend that you begin assimilating. To do so, memorize the following rules.

You are your "Work."

You must always be busy (at least look busy) and pretend to do some essential work.

Language

Never, speak in any language other than American English, no matter with whom you are talking. Unlike Europeans and Indians, speaking a foreign language is un-American. There is an exception—Spanish, but only when you have no choice.

Rewire your brain

Pay no attention to other nations and the international community, unless they happen to support the U.S. views. The majority is not always right, and logic is not eternally desirable or safe. Amidst the tremendous political ambiguity, stick with the securest stance, "the U.S.A. is always right."

Relearn world history and cultures.

Discard what you know of a non-American version of world history. Replace the works of Omar Khayyam, Rabindranath Tagore, C.V. Raman, Confucius and Chanakya with a book on guns, an album on autos showing the collected works of General Motors and Ford Motors, and "Destinations of a Lifetime," a book by National Geographic.

Always be inclusive.

When in the company of your new fellow citizens, invariably use "we" instead of "I." This may help remind them that you are part of the country. If you are not white, this tactic will not stop the daily question, "Where are you from?" I suggest you prepare a carefully drafted, thirty seconds elevator pitch to answer appropriately.

Watching July 4 fireworks at the Bay Shore Boulevard in Tampa, I could not hold back my excitement. "Fascinating! Great Show!" I said to a young man standing next to me. He smiled and stared at me for a moment and then replied, "Yeah. We, Americans, like it."

About the Author

Satish Mehta was born in New Delhi, India. He received his Bachelor of Science in electrical engineering at B.I.T.S. (Birla Institute of Technology and Science), at Pilani, Rajasthan, India and his MBA (Masters in Business Administration) from The Southern Illinois University, Carbondale, IL, USA. He came to the U.S. for two years and has stayed ever since.

Satish Mehta now works as an author, speaker, and business coach.

Connect with Me

https://satishmehtausa.wordpress.com/
https://www.amazon.com/author/satishmehta
@satishmehtausa
www.linkedin.com/in/satishmehtausa
https://www.facebook.com/satishmehtaus/